In memory of my Dad

I'm sure this book will make you laugh!

I think about you every day.

CHiPS aNd SauSage

A GuiDe to IreLaNd aNd Her WoNders

Daniel Zuchowski

Illustrated by Gemma Quevedo

Literary Publishing

Dublin 2017

Contents

Introduction

Geography

Typical Irish Family

Irish Names

Irish Holidays

Irish People on Holiday

Music

Literature

Education

Irish Cuisine

Sport

Work Ethic

Politeness

Language

Tourist Mistakes

Introduction

This book is a tribute to the Irish people, to Ireland's rich cultural heritage, and to that breathtakingly beautiful and always incredibly green land.

It can also serve as a guide to anyone who would like to learn more about Ireland and the Irish way of life.

None of the many overgeneralisations present in this book aims to offend anyone.

I love you, Ireland!

Daniel

Geography

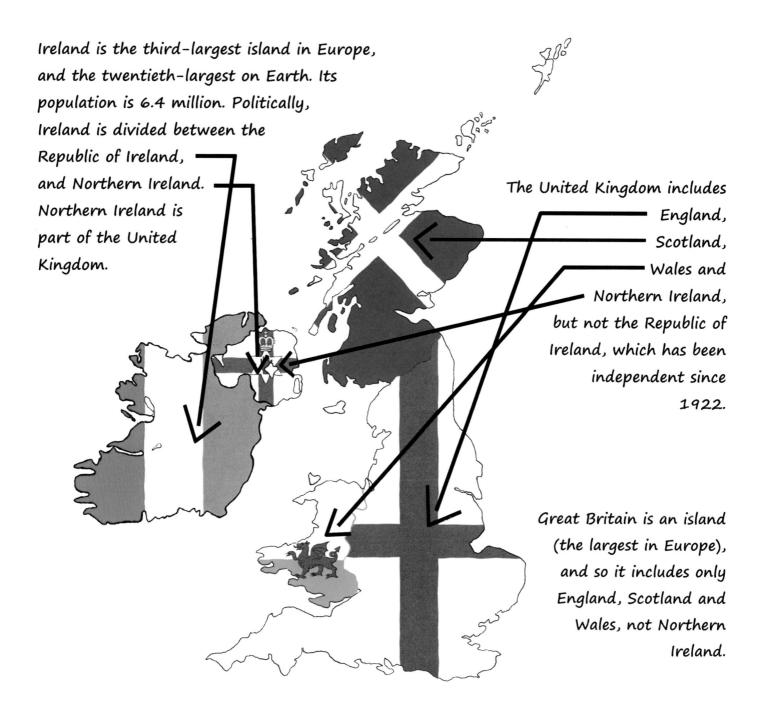

Ireland is the third-largest island in Europe, and the twentieth-largest on Earth. Its population is 6.4 million. Politically, Ireland is divided between the Republic of Ireland, and Northern Ireland. Northern Ireland is part of the United Kingdom.

The United Kingdom includes England, Scotland, Wales and Northern Ireland, but not the Republic of Ireland, which has been independent since 1922.

Great Britain is an island (the largest in Europe), and so it includes only England, Scotland and Wales, not Northern Ireland.

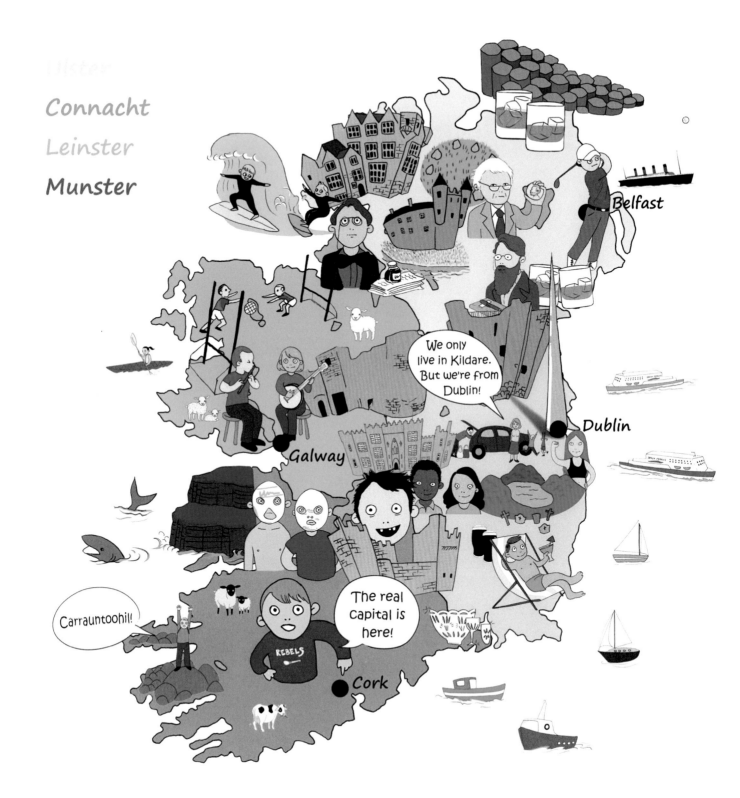

Typical Irish Family

semi-detached
house

three sweet kids

or terraced house

two cars

(Opel, VW or Citroen for her;

BMW or Audi for him)

two loving parents
(same-sex permissible)

or four sweet kids

dog

(optional; over a third of
Irish households own a dog)

au pair

or five sweet kids

IriSH NaMeS

Tadhg   Méabh

Eoin   Aoife   Ruaidhri   Niamh

These are some of the more popular Irish names. But don't even try to pronounce them. You'll fail miserably no matter how hard you go for it.

Irish Holidays

Except for St. Patrick's Day (17th March), no other Irish-specific holidays exist.

The main St. Patrick's Day parade takes place in Dublin, but most Dubliners try to flee as far away as possible, often ending up celebrating this holiday in one of the 7000 Irish pubs abroad. (Yes, the number of Irish pubs outside of Ireland is almost equal to that in Ireland.)

NOTE: St. Patrick's Day does not commemorate Leprechauns. Well, at least it didn't use to... It used to be a Catholic holiday which celebrated the life and accomplishments of St. Patrick (the bloke who in the 5th century brought Christianity to then-pagan Ireland). These days, though, 17th March is just a day when Irish people celebrate their culture and heritage.

Irish People on Holiday

MUSiC

Irish people love music

Music is everywhere in Ireland. Many pubs have live music every night (and some even during the day), and in other pubs you can stumble upon an informally organised 'session', where local music enthusiasts gather together to share their passion for traditional Irish tunes.

'Session' is also a term used in Ireland to refer to a situation where large quantities of alcohol are consumed in a social setting. Therefore, 'The session was mighty!' could mean that the music was cool, or that you had a great craic partying and drinking — or both.

Oh, and 'craic' roughly translates to 'good time'.

Literature

In Ireland, you will never find a house without books.
Irish people love reading, and they are very proud of their literary tradition.

Education

Ireland ranks very high in third-level education surveys. Between the years 2000-2010, the percentage of people with a college degree in Ireland nearly doubled. But that's not all. Irish people in general are very well-read and well-travelled, which means that talking to them is (almost) always a pleasure.

Irish Cuisine

Sport

Gaelic football

Yes, that's right – you can catch the ball! And you can run with it, too!
But don't forget to bounce it, or kick it, after four steps.

Hurling

The oldest and fastest game on grass.
And yes, the sliothar (the ball) is as hard as a stone.

Work Ethic

Irish people love holidays! (Well, who doesn't...) But in contrast to other European nations, they don't all tend to take their annual leave in August. They like to take their holidays at different times of the year, e.g. in January, to escape the cold. Who would like to leave Ireland in the beautiful months of summer anyway?!

POLiTeNeSS

They care about how you are

They apologise even if it's not their fault

With the exception of Dublin, where most of your neighbours probably won't even acknowledge your existence

They love socialising

Later...

It's a land of a thousand welcomes
(céad míle fáilte) and...
a thousand goodbyes

And frequent F-words

Language

Irish accent often comes top in accent surveys

We're sure you've
seen one of them silly surveys.

'Me' (object pronoun) in place of 'my' (possessive adjective)

The past simple form of 'break' ('broke') instead of the past participle ('broken')

Singular form of the verb 'to be' after 'there'

Immediate perfective ("I was just after finishing college" instead of the more standard "I had just finished college")

Non-standard 'like'

Irish youth like to take a gap year. And we recommend it to everyone! Just look how well-travelled and well-read young Irish people are.

Peadar has the dinner prepared...

Resultative perfective (object + past participle word order instead of the more standard past participle + object, as in 'Peadar has prepared the dinner.'

Inverted word order in reported questions (more standard: '...and then he asked me if I was hungry!').

Lack of 'do' and 'got' in have-questions

'Ya', 'ye', 'youse', 'yeez' are all different forms of the singular or plural second-person pronoun

'Locked' and 'plastered' are two of the 150 words that Irish people have for 'drunk'

Tourist Mistakes

Visiting Ireland in January

Renting a car without full insurance and driving it in the countryside

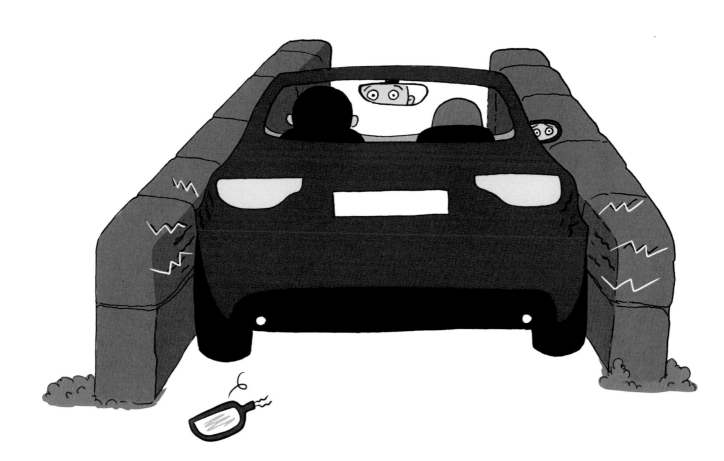

Travelling to all little castles around Ireland
(here, Malahide Castle), but...

...never visiting Dublin Castle and its secret gardens

Thinking Guinness is the only "black beer"

Many other breweries also make stout ("black beer"). Apart from Guinness, there are Murphy's, Beamish, O'Hara's, and more! Sláinte!

Believing that a leprechaun and St. Patrick are the same thing

Trying to buy alcohol in a shop after 22.00 and before 10.30
(12.30 on Sundays)

Trying to buy alcohol in a shop on St. Patrick's Day

On 17th March (St. Patrick's Day), alcohol can only be bought in pubs and restaurants. But drinking in public is allowed on this special day.

ALCOHOL MAY NOT BE PURCHASED TODAY 17th MARCH

Published by Literary Publishing in Dublin in 2017
www.literarypublishinghouse.com
@literarypub

First edition
ISBN: 978-0-9928132-3-9

Illustrated by Gemma Quevedo

@ChipsAndSausage

Made in the USA
Middletown, DE
31 October 2017